MW01114780

In Search of the Divine

In Search of the Divine

John R. Powers

RESOURCE *Publications* · Eugene, Oregon

IN SEARCH OF THE DIVINE

Copyright © 2021 John R. Powers. All rights reserved. Except for brief
quotations in critical publications or reviews, no part of this book may
be reproduced in any manner without prior written permission from the
publisher. Write: Permissions, Wipf and Stock Publishers, 199 W. 8th Ave.,
Suite 3, Eugene, OR 97401.

Resource Publications
An Imprint of Wipf and Stock Publishers
199 W. 8th Ave., Suite 3
Eugene, OR 97401

www.wipfandstock.com

PAPERBACK ISBN: 978-1-6667-2336-6
HARDCOVER ISBN: 978-1-6667-2004-4
EBOOK ISBN: 978-1-6667-2005-1

08/27/21

Contents

Preface

Since the beginning of recorded history, men and women have experienced a profound longing for a connection beyond themselves. This is well embodied in Augustine's "our heart is restless until it finds it's rest in thee." We sense that there is something profound that is missing in our lives but it is something for which we have no clear idea how to find it nor how to recognize it if we do find it.

In the West, we tend to seek it in religious institutions most notably the one that is centered around the earthly ministry of a Nazarene in the first century AD. What is known about this Nazarene, however, has been so redacted that it impedes our search and renders the value of the services offered in his name questionable. As a result, many have walked away from these services especially in Europe.

"In Search of the Divine" does not pretend to provide a roadmap to a definitive search. It does, however, provide hints that can lead to experiences of the transcendent. These hints include options that only require that we be receptive of what is there. These options include the scriptures of the Old and New Testaments but these will be useful only if we see them not as special revelation but as writings by men and women who struggled with the ultimate questions in life and immersed themselves in the search for the divine.

The problem with these scriptures is that they were assigned an inspired status that they never were intended to be given and this gets in the way of their utility. Freeing them, however, will require a whole new theological foundation that does away with these affirmations and presents the scriptures as what they have always been; writings by deeply devout men and women.

In addition to our need to find fulfilment by experiencing the divine, we often seek relief from the vicissitudes in life. We can feel overwhelmed by the negatives we encounter such as unwelcome natural phenomena, bad outcomes at work or rejections in relationships often as a result of our own doing. The most serious distress that we receive is when we recognize our own mortality. Over the centuries, these have provided openings for practitioners who offer solutions in the form of petitions, sacrifices and rituals.

Once these practitioners garner adherents, spawn more practitioners and form sects they create belief systems that can obscure our search for the divine. While many of these sects are formed with the purist of motives, ultimately, they are commercial enterprises that must break even and to do so must provide concrete answers to the mysteries of our lives. As a result, we get attuned to the notion that this is where we will encounter the divine.

Alternatively, consider Herman Hesse's Siddhartha. He tried many different paths none of which proved satisfying but each path expanded his being and provided insights into his universe in which he was living. It is in this spirit that we go forth boldly in search of the divine by freeing ourselves from the strictures that bind us, becoming one with others and experiencing the transcendent.

"In Search for the Divine" seeks to address these issues, challenge current theologies and provide hints to pathways by which we may experience the transcendent and expand our lives, benefit our communities and lead to insights that will benefit all we touch.

In Search of the Divine

WE HAVE AN INHERENT longing to connect to a transcendent reality outside of ourselves. This longing, however, takes so many forms that we will never really understand it. We can, however, observe its many manifestations and find ways to connect.

In many ways, mainstream Christianity is not very helpful because of the way it is wedded to unsustainable notions of an inspired Bible. Yet the Bible should not be discarded but seen as an unparalleled guide in the search for the divine. This, however, will require a new theological foundation that expands rather than diminishes our search.

Since the beginning of time, mankind has experienced a profound longing for a connection beyond our selves. This is well represented by Augustine's "our heart is restless until it finds it's rest in thee." This longing is also found in mankind's angst when confronted by the vicissitudes of daily living.

The problem with the latter is that it creates practitioners who offer ways to control these forces through petitions, rituals and sacrifices. These vicissitudes include not only destructive natural phenomena but also the negatives we encounter in our studies, work and relationships that are often the result of our own doing. Add to this, the ultimate trauma we experience when we become face to face with our own mortality.

These practitioners garner adherents that spawn more practitioners and from this process, religious communitys are formed that often impede rather than facilitate the search for the divine.

They do this by attempting to represent the divine in closed form rather than acknowledging the fact that we really know very little about the divine and need to be open to whatever forms the divine might be presented to us and by which we might connect.

Herman Hesse's Siddhartha[1] is an excellent illustration of the search with no closure but with an expansion of his own being thru the process of the search. It is in this spirit that we go forth boldly searching these many manifestations in the desire to experience the transcendent and become one with others.

The major concern is when these needs are harnessed by practitioners to produce theologies that will not square with experience. We all screw up badly at times and in many of these instances there may not be a do-over. Yet, we are often promised that with enough faith this is possible but when the results are not as hoped it is because "God" has other plans for us. Ultimately, we need to acknowledge that we are largely on our own with no benevolent power looking after us.

Further, included in these questionable theologies are imbedded value and behavioral systems that we are asked to incorporate into our personal lives. It is the effects of these that need careful examination.

- Do they enhance our quality of life and that of our communities or

- Do they degrade our quality of life and that of our communities?

The unfortunate aspect of value and behavioral systems created by the practitioners is that many have very harmful consequences. As is often the case, the framing of these value and behavioral systems by the practitioners is in the service of their own personal, social, financial, and professional needs. The selling of indulgences and Jonestown Cult are among the most outrageous examples but the religious landscape is rife with lesser examples

1. Herman Hesse, Siddhartha, Sherab Chodzin Kohn (translator), Shambhala, 2000.

that take advantage of parishioners. We will come back to this later. First, we must look at the bigger picture.

The Longing and its Impact

The longing that drives our search for the divine seems to have originated from a) the mystery of our own being and b) the vicissitudes of our daily lives. The former is one of the great imponderables and yet is a key ingredient in the formulation of many of our religious religious communitys and rituals. In some cases, these have a capacity of lifting us out of ourselves in a way that we can experience an unbounded moment in what we perceive as a transcendent reality.

It is the latter, the vicissitudes of our daily lives that seem to play the largest role of the formulation of religious communities and the evolution of values and behaviors systems so we will concentrate on these.

It has been deduced from scant but solid evidence that the earliest peoples felt vulnerable to the forces of nature and created a pantheon of deities to give some hope that these forces could be controlled through petitions, rituals and sacrifices. These deities included those for sky, sun, moon, water, forests, hearth, fire along with others associated with naturally occurring phenomena such as wind, rain, thunder, fertility, et al.

These deities, individually and in constellations, had practitioners who benefited by converting individual and communal needs into rites and rituals. In a remote village in Nepal in the shadow of Dhaulagiri, one of our porters became ill and the head Sherpa found a shaman who performed a healing ritual in a tent using incantations along with tossing sparkling substances into a fire. The porter felt better and the shaman received a small stipend for his efforts.

It is a historical fact that practitioners of all stripes gain converts and the resultant gaining of converts spawn additional practitioners. The practitioners along with their converts can then evolve into a religious community that codifies the rites and rituals along with tenets, values and behaviors that assure the status of the religious community and undergird the position of the practitioners. Once the religious community has become established, it becomes extremely competitive as in Exodus 20:20 (thou shalt have no other gods before me). This commandment does not say, "I am the one true God." It says that "if you are to be my followers and belong to my community of believers, then you shall not patronize any of my rival gods."

This process of religious community formation is not limited to responses to physical needs such as rain in the midst of a multi-year drought but has often included the revulsion of social reformers to abhorrent social conditions. The brief public tenure of a Nazarene in the first century and a German professor of theology in the sixteenth are excellent cases in point. Both appear to have been motivated not by personal gain but by a zeal to right the societal wrongs imbedded in the dominant religious structures of their times as they perceived them.

Both of these reformers articulated new ways of behaving but the focus of their messages was quite different. The Nazarene was primarily speaking to the people with a focus on how they were to live whereas the German was addressing the religious hierarchy of the time. Both, of course, gained large number of converts but the subsequent evolution of their converts into religious communities differed widely.

In the case of the German, his primary impact was to break the dam of control maintained by the then dominant religious hierarchy and to produce a flood of religious thinkers not wedded to the tenets of that hierarchy. This produced a movement that in turn resulted in an innumerable number of different religious communities each with similar but with often distinct tenets.

One of the major problems created by the break from the then dominant hierarchy was that it left an authoritative vacuum that had previously provided order by serving as the ultimate authority in the resolution of differences in "faith and morals." In the absence of any other option, the Bible was enlisted to fill that vacuum. In order for it to fulfill this role, however, it could not simply be a collection of human writings so its stature was increased to that of an inspired document and then one that is infallible.

It was pretty much regarded as such until the early part of the twentieth century when it ran into the scientific evidence regarding the creation of the universe and the origin of the human species. Earlier notables such as Jefferson had pointed out some of its inconsistencies and contradictions but their views did not get a widespread distribution and these views did not have much of an impact. Thus, in the middle of the nineteenth century, protestant theologians such as Charles Hodge were able to erect monumental theological tomes based on an infallible Bible.[2]

The conflict between the biblical and the emerging scientific theories came to a head in 1925 when John Scopes was put on trial in Tennessee for teaching evolution. The central issue was whether the "Word of God" as revealed in the Bible took priority over all human knowledge. While the creation stories were somewhat irrelevant to the central tenets of Christianity, the Scopes' notion implied the possibility that the Bible not only contained factual errors but could simply be a compilation of human writings.

This was such a serious challenge to the Bible's status that even into the later part of the twentieth century, some candidates for ordination were required to subscribe to an infallible Bible (in some cases, however, there was some wiggle room by applying that only to faith and morals).

This struggle over the status of the Bible persisted into the twenty first century as shown by Alexandra Pelosi's 2007 documentary, "Friends of God," that can be seen on YouTube. Her documentary vividly showed the extent to which fundamentalists would go in bending the minds of young children and their adult adherents to the belief in an infallible Bible.

As a consequence, one must ask, why is this conflict over the introductory religious community on on cosmology (Genesis 1:1 to 2:4a) and the creation of the human species (Genesis 2:4b to 3:24) so important? Nothing we do in our daily lives hangs on the correctness of either of the competing theories. The answer lay in

2. Charles Hodge, Systematic Theology, Hendrickson Publishers, 1999.

the centrality of the Christian message contained in John 3:16, "For God so loved the world, that he gave his only begotten Son, that whoever believes in Him shall not perish, but have everlasting life." This and similar passages address what many consider to be the most formidable trauma we experience in our lives: the recognition of our own mortality.

This recognition creates an underlying dread that becomes a factor in the whole of our lives unless we can find a resolution that will reduce this dread. While this dread is not the most immediate of the challenges we experience, it is by far the most powerful. Think here of the large number of people who refer to deceased family and friends as "passed" rather than "dead." For this reason, the resolution of the dread of our own mortality provides the central benefit of many of the higher-level religious communities throughout history.

We can now see why it was essential for the fundamentalists to hold the line on the inerrancy of the Genesis accounts. If these portions of the canon were accepted as contrivances on the part of the Israeli priests for the purpose of establishing the authority for the observance of the Sabbath (Genesis 1:1 to 2:4a) or just oral tradition handed down by ancient story tellers to explain the origin of sin and the primacy of the male gender (Genesis 2:4b to 3:24), then what assurance would the adherents have in the veracity of a contract that would assure eternal life. The obvious answer, of course, is none.

We know that the Bible is replete with inaccuracies and contradictions. The early Roman Church recognized this and did its best to keep the Bible away from its followers. In the splintering that is known as the Reformation, dodges were created to blunt the impact of these inaccuracies. For a long time, these scriptures were seen as the Word of God or "special revelation." When that was no longer tenable, the Bible shifted from being the Word of God to containing the Word of God.

The emphasis then became "having faith" which was code for putting away questions and doubts and relying on the words of the practitioners. As a teen, I asked questions of my pastor and was told that "you will understand better when you are older." I am now older and perhaps wiser for having graduated with an MDiv from Princeton Theological Seminary and having served three years in pastoral vocations before earning a PhD in Physics from Penn.

I will return to the questions of the authenticity of the Christian scriptures later and will try to establish that they are what they appear to be: the products of deeply devoted men and women but nonetheless products of the human mind in response to their environment as they encountered it. I would say the same about the Norse, Greek and Roman pantheons as well as the scriptures of all of the contemporary religions.

The Pathways

The absence of authoritative scriptures forces us to take a very different look at our individual searches for the divine. While it does not diminish experiences of religious rapture inside or outside of houses of worship, it does force us to consider them differently. Clearly, these experiences have an intrinsic value for those individuals experiencing such moments but there are obviously no criteria with which one can validate or invalidate personal experiences in which we are lifted out of ourselves into a plane of reality we had never previously experienced.

This perspective has to be applied to all personal experiences that can be described as rapturous. We see this often in evangelical settings during an alter call in which the worshipper is called upon to commit to Jesus for the forgiveness of sins and promise of everlasting life. These experiences are well documented and in many cases are life changing. Converts who have born devastating guilt can be freed and, in some cases, alcoholics are transformed. We also see parishioners swept up in the emotions of a dynamic service in which the whole of a congregation is moved as one. Augustine's "my heart is restless until it finds it's rest in thee" is a testament to the healing power of these transforming experiences.

There are two things, however, that over time tend to erode the value of these experiences: a) the return to the mundane and b) unsustainability of the theological foundations upon which the bliss was based. Consider the return to the mundane. One of the most idyllic experiences in my life was a two-week Christian camp in a bucolic environment in rural Maryland. My teen years were not happy years and the camp was the antithesis of everything that seemed to be wrong in my peer relationships.

Even on the drive home I could envision life becoming fundamentally different. It was as if the Kingdom of God was at hand: a state that can be achieved here on earth. In my mind it had nothing to do with an afterlife and everything to do with the immediate. The problem was that within two days of my return home, I sank back into the lows of my peer relationships.

The Tyranny of the Mundane

The central question related to the search for the divine becomes "how does a transcendent experience integrate with the whole of one's life." In my case after my return from church camp, the answer was "not very well." The potential conflict between the transcendent and the mundane is a paradox as the transcendent experience is apart from the whole of one's life and yet it needs somehow to impact that life.

Consider, then, the reemergence from the Christian camp experience back to the conflict driven world of the teen. In just two days, I went from the highs of the camp to the lows of the neighborhood. The question here is not the authenticity of the camp experience but rather how the rapture can be sustained.

The answer, sadly, is "with great difficulty." There are, however, some observations that can be used with a skillful analysis of the dynamics of the camp and that of the neighborhood for the purpose of narrowing the difference. In this pursuit, we are looking for ways in which the neighborhood can be made more like the camp or for ways of making the camp more like the neighborhood.

Let's first deal with making the camp more like the neighborhood as it is the easier of the two.

One way that has been employed successfully is mission trips in which the focus of the camp is meeting the needs of the neighborhood. Working in the inner city to meet some of the almost countless needs of the residents is one such option. It could be as simple as working with the neighbors in a clean-up effort or as demanding as tutoring children who are way behind in school. Another way is to structure the camp around a select set of shared needs emerging from the neighborhood. A third possibility would be requiring each camper bring at least one close friend from her or his neighborhood.

The more difficult task will be to make the neighborhood more like the camp. For me, that would have required that I eliminate my then current relationships and go solo for a while looking for new ones. This would be hard for any adult to do by oneself and would be particularly hard for a teen. *One way to get started in this direction is to have a session in the camp in which each of the attendees articulate clearly what she or he really wants out of life (as goals) and then develop a detailed approach for how to get from where one is at that moment to where one wants to be.* This suggests the next step that is closely akin to Cognitive Behavioral Therapy (CBT) where the leader can isolate both the goals and the ways the person is now using her or himself to achieve that goal and then ask, "How well is what you are doing now working toward the fulfillment of your stated goals?" In my case, such an approach would have revealed a huge disconnect.

This could take place at the camp but it would be extremely difficult for most camps to provide. Camps (religious and otherwise) are activity oriented and are geared to a large number of people whereas much of the above would require one-on-one interactions. Yet, the approach is fairly straightforward, each of the individuals could take this to a supportive setting after camp. One possible source might be the Church but few pastors or church members are focused on doing this nor are they trained sufficiently.

It is possible, however that a church could form groups with qualified leaders but this is beyond the scope of most churches.

Whether this approach would be sufficient to overcome the "tyranny of the mundane" is an open question as there are additional potential barriers that could get in the way particularly if the camp experience is based on a religious perspective that doesn't square with reality.

Unsustainable Theological Foundations

Overcoming the tyranny of the mundane after a rapturous experience may be problematic if the rapture is based on fraudulent theological assumptions. There is a very dynamic preacher who broadcasts weekly who has an unparalleled understanding of human psychology. His sermons are almost all on point with respect to the exigencies of our daily lives and he articulates extremely well the challenges that we all face as we toil in our work places and try do our best as parents, spouses, employees, friends and neighbors.

The problem arises when he follows his prescient descriptions of our travails with the comforting words that we should not fret as all of this is in God's plan for us. Yes, it is a huge plus that we adopt a positive outlook in the face of troubles. This gives us an edge in being able to resolve our most serious problems successfully and there are even some medical studies that have shown the benefits of faith in the helping hand of God. Nonetheless, he is making promises in the name of God for which he might not be able to deliver.

It might be useful to chart the statistics of promises versus outcomes but that would be seen as undercutting faith and could affect outcomes. I remember many sermons that touted ". . . if you have faith as small as a mustard seed, you can say to this mountain, 'Move from here to there,' and it will move. Nothing will be impossible for you (Matthew 17:20)." I am not sure how this made its way into the cannon but it is clear that not a whole lot of mountains have been moved by faith in the past twenty centuries. Even if we take this as hyperbole ascribed to Jesus, for most of us, the success rate in achieving results thru faith has not been very good.

This suggests that we need a totally new theological foundation that is not based on scriptural passages that were added by practitioners long after Jesus died for the purpose of elevating his status and sustaining the institutions that were being built on his name. We will come back to the authority of scripture shortly but in considering the motivations of the practitioners, there is an insight that merits attention seen in a PBS series titled "Rick Steves' Europe." In almost every episode, Steves tours gigantic edifices built from the middle ages thru modern times. It is hard to imagine the price that was paid by the faithful in producing these magnificent structures while barely being able to eke out a living sufficient to house, feed and clothe their families. Yet, the purpose in building them is inescapable.

The primary purpose of these edifices is to create awe in the minds of the populace for the purposes of a) reinforcing the pre-eminence of the religion of their builders and b) lifting individuals into a transcendental experience. While the first is somewhat suspect the second serves a very important existential purpose. The real issue here is how to harness the positive aspects of a transcendental experience in these edifices and avoid the traps of the practitioner builders.

While our churches have the potential of actually assisting us in experiencing the transcendent and in helping integrate these experiences with our daily lives, we need to understand that the practitioners who head these institutions are the heads of commercial enterprises that need to at least break even to sustain themselves. I have a dear friend who came out of Seminary very close theologically to the views being expressed here. In the interim years, he has become the pastor of a major 1000-person church and now sounds very much like pastor who told me when I was a teen that I would understand better when I was older. The commercial needs of his profession eventually cooped him.

From this perspective, churches can be a mixed blessing. Yes, we can gain from church experiences but we need to remember that the mission, vision, values and goals of these churches may be different than ours.

Transcendent Experiences

We need to clarify what we mean by a "transcendent experience." Traditionally, this is taken as an experience that takes one out of oneself and points to a larger reality. I would thus classify as such an experience I had during the early hours of an evening camped at 17,800 feet on Mara La in the Himalayas. There were zero outside lights and no moon obscuring my view of the unbelievable majesty of the universe. Whether I had touched the face of God or was simply suffering from oxygen deprivation I will never know but the experience itself was expanding, awe inspiring and thereby transcendent.

I would have to apply the same uncertainty to social experiences including romantic experiences in which we are lifted out of ourselves into a plane of reality we had never previously experienced. I do believe that the author of 1 John 4:7 had an important insight when he wrote, "let us love one another, for love comes from God. Everyone who loves has been born of God and knows God." The love here is usually translated as a "pure, willful, sacrificial love that intentionally desires another's highest good."

This illustrates beautifully the difficulty in speaking about God. The Westminster divines in 1648[3] tried to help by stating that "God is a Spirit, in and of himself infinite in being, glory, blessedness, and perfection; all-sufficient, eternal, unchangeable, incomprehensible, everywhere present, almighty, knowing all things, most wise, most holy, most just, most merciful and gracious, long-suffering, and abundant in goodness and truth." This has been shortened to read, "God is a spirit, whose being, wisdom, power, holiness, justice, goodness, and truth are infinite, eternal,

---

3. The Westminster Larger Catechism (1648) by Westminster Divines, https://www.ligonier.org/learn/articles/westminster-larger-catechism/

and unchangeable."[4] In either case, this is simply verbiage and not very helpful.

At least the Westminster divines did repudiate the anthropomorphic images as in Michelangelo's ceiling in the Sistine Chapel but this vignette makes clear two things: a) practitioners will create verbiage when stuck for answers and b) we really don't know much if anything about the object of our search for the divine or even if God can be considered an object of our search. While we can echo Descartes famous, "I think therefore I am," we cannot say, "I am the whole of everything." So, we can be confident that there is a reality beyond our own being.

We do know the things we can see, touch, hear, smell and taste but we do sense that there is something more. This sense seems to have driven the path of Hermann Hesse's Siddhartha in his search for spiritual illumination.[5] Siddhartha begins by becoming a wandering ascetic beggar and continues along several very different paths somewhat related to conventional eastern religious practices. The take away seems to be that there is never closure; only a continued search. Ultimately, we are driven by the need to continually search.

Unlike Siddhartha, however, most of us do not have the wherewithal to devote the whole of our lives to the search. Instead, we must toil at our daily tasks consisting of earning a living, raising a family, serving our communities and engaging in many other activities. In the midst of all of this, there is a gnawing need to search for the divine. In part, practitioners have established institutions to meet aspects of this need and many find a level of fulfillment as a result.

Again, it is unknown whether the vast diversity in theological foundations says anything about the validity of the outcomes presented by these many different practitioners. While Ernest Becker,[6] would consign most of these to an inauthentic existence,

---

4. Westminster Shorter Catharism, https://learnscripture.net/catechisms/WSCME/.

5. Hermann Hesse, Op Cit.

6. Ernst Becker, *Denial of Death*, The Free Press, 1973

we really cannot endorse that view. This can only be judged by the way in which the outcomes translate back into the lives of the individuals (outcomes being the impact of a personal transcendental experiences on the whole of a person's life).

Since we have acknowledged that there are many different forms these can take, let's consider a couple: a) a conversion experience of a homeless alcoholic and b) the rapturous experience when a lonely woman feels she is loved for the first time.

The homeless alcoholic became a homeless alcoholic for many different reasons that may have included broken relationships, bad deeds, unfortunate circumstances that she or he was unable to cope, gambling debts, etc., etc. The conversion experience will certainly be euphoric and will produce an instantaneous changed mindset that can be extremely powerful. This is all to the benefit of the woman or man struggling with the depths of despair. At issue is its sustainability. The chances of long-term success without hands on support are not that good. We cannot criticize the efficaciousness of the transcendental experience as the person emerging from it emerges with all the right motivations to do what is necessary to right her or his life. Unfortunately, it is unlikely that a single experience over a scant period of time can correct years of cumulative problems without a lot of continued support such as alcoholics anonymous or a rehab center. The person, however, may need financial aid that a church might provide.

The lonely woman or man who really feels loved for the first time is having a very different type of a transcendental experience, Nonetheless, this person has experienced a level of euphoria that can be unprecedented for that person. This is where the 1 John 4:7 (. . . love one another . . . everyone who loves . . . knows God) is so profound. For some, this momentary transient in life, can be considered by this person as having, metaphorically, seen the face of God.

In this momentary instant, this person has experienced "possibility." Our greatest need in this modern world is for such profound human relationships. Establishing "profound relationships" is not, however, an easy task. Moments of rapturous love can be followed by a descent into the pits. Sartre's "hell is other people"[7] through abuse or disappointment abounds sufficiently that this merits serious concern. Notwithstanding, we must venture forth courageously or we will never get beyond the mundane in life.

We can have no quibble with individual experiences perceived as transcendent regardless of the location and the events that triggered it. There is a great utility in attendance in houses of worship as potential venues for lifting us there. I had one such experience attending a magical mass at Saint Mary's seminary, a Jesuit school in Kansas and an equally powerful experience joining in the rapture at a black Baptist church in New Jersey. Each of these experiences lifted me beyond the mundane and, thereby, can be considered a glimpse of the divine.

Such experiences can and will vary widely. So much so that we might consider our search for the divine much like that of the blind men in the Hindu parable in which they each touch a different part of an elephant (first reported in the Buddhist text, Udana 6.4). In some versions, each of the men comes to believe his perception is the absolute truth and the rest are flawed and thus sets out to convince the others that his was the true vision.

We need to look beyond the surface of this parable into why there is a need to convince others. If the motive is only for self-assurance that his is the true vision, then the energy expended will not be that great. If, however, each of the blind men had been able to find believers in their individual perceptions, then, as their followers multiply, practitioners multiply and a religious community is formed. This begins the need to convince others. This need becomes of prime importance as the practitioners of each religious community are dependent on being the keepers of the true vision, the inevitable competition ensues and the religious community does what it needs to do to sustain itself.

It is a sad truth that once the collection of followers becomes a religious community, it quickly takes on all of the characteristics of a business, its principal goal becomes sustaining that business and protecting the practitioner's income. This, however, is not to

---

7. Jean Paul Sartre, No Exit and Three Other Plays, Vintage, 1989

say that the practitioners are bad people. Virtually every one of my fellow students at the Princeton Theological Seminary entered with a vision of serving others with the most altruistic motives. The problems arise as their economic needs press upon them and the force of some powerful parishioners' desires for a particular set of beliefs from the pulpit push them into uncomfortable positions.

An unsavory example was highlighted in the Pelosi Friends of God documentary.[8] Ted Haggard was the President of the National Association of Evangelicals until a few days after the shooting of the documentary. He was a staunch advocate for everything biblical including its antipathy to homosexuality. Despite his outward piety, he was dismissed from his church for "sexually immoral conduct" reportedly for having sex with a male prostitute.

The point here is not his giving in to his sexual needs but the hypocrisy inherent in his strong advocacy of the Bible's inerrancy necessary to sustain the evangelical wing of Protestantism, its view of homosexuality and his paycheck. This is what was at the heart of my pastor's response to me when I was a teen. He must have been terribly threatened by my questions as he must have asked them himself many times. He was, however, in a terrible bind. He was in his early forties and the only professional credentials he held was as a minister. I have seen this too often among my former Seminary colleagues.

It is something to be wished that these practitioners would be sympathetic to an approach based on a Bible as an inspirational document but devoid of all of its authoritative claims. The Bible could then become an invaluable resource in the search for the divine along with the development of values and behavioral systems that enhance the quality of our lives. Ironically, this was what Jesus sought to do as an itinerant preacher seeking to lead others into enhancing the quality of their lives and those of their neighbors. This approach, however, would get most pastors tossed out on their ear by the sessions of their employing churches.

In order to succeed in ministry, a pastor must present her or his congregation concrete products. The then President of

8. Alexandra Pelosi, op cit.

Princeton Theological Seminary was wise enough to understand this when he made it clear in a presentation at an alumni reunion. He asserted that "Princeton Seminary is not a school of religion like that in the neighboring Princeton University, the Seminary is a confessional institution." The seminary's job, as understood by this President, was not to turn out searchers for the divine but practitioners who would sustain the denomination by providing concrete constructs and guidance to congregations.

Schopenhauer would argue that there is no God to be comprehended.[9] Tillich would frame this in terms of a rather squishy, "ultimate concern."[10] As far apart as these two appear, these pretty much add up to the same thing. When we speak of God, we have absolutely no idea what we are talking about. It is a totally subjective experience that can only be articulated thru poetic images. This, to repeat, does not invalidate the search.

If we have no idea what we are talking about when we speak of God, then how did these religious constructs emerge that are represented by mammoth arrays of tenets. This is the unsettling part of this query. As suggested above, these constructs emerged to undergird the religious edifices in which they were found.

Consider the ransom theory of Gregory of Nyssa in the fourth century. In this theory, God tricks the devil into a ransom exchange: Jesus' death in exchange for freeing humanity from its bondage in sin. "The divinity of Jesus is like the hook, which also gets swallowed by death, much to the surprise of the devil" and overpowers the darkness of death because "it is not in the nature of darkness to remain when light is present or of death to exist when life is active."[11]

This seemed to be the prevalent thought as the early church was emerging and defining itself. The notions of sacrifice as a means of placating the deity were still alive in most of the world's

9. Schopenhauer. https://plato.stanford.edu/entries/schopenhauer/, May 2003

10. Paul Tillich, Dynamics of Faith, Harper and Brothers, 1958

11. Catechism of the Catholic Church, http://www.scborromeo.org/ccc/para/494.htm

religions at the time. In the emerging church, one of the requirements for Jesus' sacrifice to be efficacious was for Jesus to be without sin. Since original sin was viewed as being transferred through the father, then Jesus had to be born of a virgin. The veneration of the Virgin persists today despite the fact that "its historical foundations are very flimsy."[12]

Throughout this early church period, the biblical records were attuned to the constructs of the church as it continued to define itself. This is why there was so many emendations of the earliest records in Q and Mark. The point is that we savor the church as a venue to experience the transcendent but question the basis of both the church's and the Bible's claims of being an authoritative source of the nature of the divine.

Since our major concern is to be able to find ways that will enhance the quality of our lives and that of our communities, we will return to that subject shortly. First, however, we need look further into the issues that show that scriptures are not only creations of human authors but were often redacted to meet the ecclesiastical needs of their times.

Authority of Scripture

In my introductory Old Testament course at Princeton Seminary, Professor James Armstrong gave us a hint into the fundamental quandary we would face upon graduation. In his commentary on Genesis 3:8, "the Lord God walked in the garden in the cool of the day," he observed that "it made sense that God would do so only during the evening as no self-respective Bedouin would walk in the open during the heat of the day." It was a strong suggestion that these passages were the natural outgrowth of human experience.

Armstrong did not, however, spell out the nature of the quandary which is "how do we preserve the central message of Christianity without the backing of a divinely inspired Bible?" Instead, he left this as an issue for future graduates to resolve.

12. The Christbook: Matthew 1–12," Bruner 2004

We must now investigate whether the Bible is as he had hinted: a collection of stories of human origin and redacted in future years to meet the then ecclesiastical needs of the practitioners. We have already spoken of Genesis 1:1 to 2:4a as written in the early part of the 6th century BCE for several purposes not the least of which was to support the priestly interest in establishing the Sabbath. Perhaps some additional examples will help:

- God grows tired and needs rest (Genesis 2:2). "So, on the seventh day, he rested from all his work. This strangely is in the initial creation story that portrays God as omnipotent and remote and much more closely aligned with the 2:4b thru the end of 3 narrative where God walks thru the garden in the cool of the evening. Yet it needs to be there to establish the no-work requirement of the Sabbath.

- Noah and the flood (Genesis 6:1 to 9:17). If the waters had risen above the top of Mount Ararat (16,854 feet or 3.24 miles above sea level) then the whole of the earth would have been under water to that depth. That's a lot of water: 638,676,962 additional cubic miles of water compared to the 332,500,000 cubic miles of water on the earth today; a factor of 1.92 additional). The obvious questions are "where did it come from; where did it go; why is there no evidence that the rest of the world below 16,854 feet had been underwater; and how did the flora and fauna across the earth below that altitude earth survive forty days under water?"

- Pharaoh's chase of the Israelites across the Red Sea (Exodus 13:17—14:29). Pharaoh's generals witnessed the parting of the sea and then made a tactical decision to pursue the Israelites into the divide. Assuming Pharaoh's generals were not total idiots, they would have recognized that if Moses could divide a sea, it would have been obvious to them that Pharaoh's forces were totally outclassed by Moses and an attack would be nothing more than suicidal. They had to have zero doubt that Moses power dwarfed theirs by several orders of magnitude. Yet they attacked. Hardly!

More to the point, however, are the miracles attributed to Jesus. The most telling fact is that Jesus got no contemporary press for these. We have mention of Jesus later in the Pauline Epistles (50 to 60 AD), Tacitus (55 AD) and Josephus (93–94 AD).[13] Yet, if these miracles had actually occurred in 30 to 33 AD, they would have made a huge splash in the histories of the time. If, as asserted, "the news was spread around the region," it would have been impossible for the Roman authorities not to have been alerted and delegations sent to investigate. Consider how extraordinary the following would have appeared to the Jewish and Roman authorities of that time.

- Healed a leper (Mark 1:40–45). "He began to talk freely . . . people came to [Jesus] from everywhere."

- Raised the widow's son from the dead (Luke 7:11–18). "This news about Jesus spread throughout Judea and the surrounding country."

- Raised the ruler's daughter from the dead (Matthew 9:18–26). "News of this spread through all that region."

- Opened the eyes of two blind men (Matthew 9:27–31). Despite Jesus request not to say anything "they . . . spread the news about him all over that region."

- Fed at least five thousand people (Matthew 14:15–21). This would have made the front page. Ditto the feeding of the four thousand.

- Raised Lazarus who was four days dead (John 11:1–46). "Some of them went to the Pharisees and told them what Jesus had done." This would have quickly reached the Jewish authorities in Jerusalem and then the Roman authorities as well.

As stated in several of these passages, if accurate, Jesus' accomplishments would have been extremely well known to both the Jewish and Roman leadership in Jerusalem, would then have

13. https://en.wikipedia.org/wiki/Sources_for_the_historicity_of_Jesus

reached the Emperor in Rome and thus to the historians at the time. Yet, there are no secular records of these or any other of Jesus' similar accomplishments. Further, if the knowledge of these events were as widespread as the texts suggest, it is certain that Herod and Pilate would have validated the "news" and would have taken a considerably different tact with him at the end. Who is going to crucify a guy with the power to do what had been attributed to him?

It is inescapable that these canonical stories are none other than later aggrandizements intended to lift Jesus' status in support of the emerging church (some of the stories rejected as outlandish in the non-canonical books were worse). Yet I am still amazed at my 93-year-old mother's insightful reaction to our reading Acts 1 and 2 as an attempt to comfort her on the evening following my father's funeral. She was emphatic, "I don't believe that stuff." This is decidedly the trend in Europe with large percentages of the population declaring themselves as non-religious. In the US, the non-religious percentage hovers around 33%. This is unfortunate and unnecessary.

Value of Scripture

The widespread rejection of scripture and the resulting rejection of the church is based largely on the fact that the practitioners elevated scriptures to a level of authority well beyond what was believable and justified. This, sadly, has been the cause of disaffections across Western Europe and more recently in the US. There is a pregnant parallel allegedly attributed to Kierkegaard as an assessment of Hegel, "if a dancer comes out on the stage and claims to leap very high and leaps very high, we applaud. If, however, he claims to fly and then only leaps very high, we mock the dancer."

The way forward is to stop touting the scriptures as if they were the inspired Word of God and by portraying them for what they are:

- Reflections by those who have searched for the divine

- Affirmations by those who felt that they knew the divine
- Constructs on the best ways to live as a part of a community
- Calls to righteousness for societies that need dramatic change
- Epistles on the foundations of the Christian faith
- Parables with powerful messages
- Just so stories to explain observed phenomena
- Possible guides to integrating the transcendent with the mundane

The scriptures are a treasure trove of great wisdom and have prompted the writing of extensive exegeses of many of its passages. While it now seems clear that they were written and collated by ordinary humans, we still need to treat them with the greatest respect. These writings can be considered on a par with those by mystics like Justin Martyr who ate roots in the desert and had visions.[14] We should take seriously his visions but not account to them any degree of authority. While we each must follow our own senses, we certainly can use the insights of those who preceded us.

We should, of course, avoid the cheat that is inherent in the attempt to redefine the scriptures' authority by using such expressions as "Heilige Geschichte (holy history)." We can probably live with expressions such as "containing the Word of God" as we do not want to dismiss the scriptures as unworthy. They indeed point to realities that are beyond our daily experiences and need to be taken seriously.

As a starter, we might try to unravel what Jesus was intending during his public ministry. He was a visionary of unequalled insight and his message should be able to stand by itself without seeing him as the Son of Man or needing to frame his teachings as more than the products of human effort. Marcus Borg does a great job in doing this in his "Meeting Jesus Again for the First Time."[15]

14. Cyril C, Richardson, Early Christian Fathers, Westminster, 1953

15. Marcus Borg, Meeting Jesus Again for the First Time, Harper One, 1995

This, of course, represents a major departure from the traditional view of the Bible. This departure, however, should not be mourned. Given the developments in higher and lower criticism and the parallel developments in secular science, it was inevitable that this would occur.

This departure, however, is not the problem. The problem is the failure of the church to develop a new view of the Bible and a new theological synthesis to take its place. There are basically four views of Scripture: the Bible is the infallible, perfect word of God (verbal inspiration); the inspired but not literal Word of God; contains the Word of God but needs to be interpreted in its historical context and demythologized; and a great and holy book but no different from other Scriptures such as the Qur'an or Upanishads.

There is really no essential difference between the last three and, ultimately, the views of the Bible can be reduced to two, namely, a view of the Bible as the "Inspired Word of God" in the strict sense and a view of the Bible that is not.

Many main stream protestants like to believe that they have found the middle ground. Unfortunately, this middle ground is a bit squishy. We try to kid ourselves that our less-than-totally inspired interpretations of the Bible are not much different than the traditional interpretation. Not so; the ultra-conservative churches have recognized the pitfalls in the less-than-totally inspired views and, as stated earlier, one major denomination made adherence to the traditional view a non-negotiable standard for ordination.

Ironically, many if not most of the denominations adhering to the traditional view seem to be flourishing. They understand their market, they know their product and the results are evident. It is beneficial, therefore, to examine their product line and the portion of the market that they are able to capture.

At its core is the notion that the text of the Bible can be taken as factual reality. Hence, their primary market is the collection of people who want and need an "infallible" Bible. We should not seek to meet this need as it will eventually flounder as has happened in Europe. We should, instead, seek to help people move beyond such needs.

The reason for this is that a religious experience based on an "infallible Bible" can become quite dysfunctional particularly where a system of a person's religious beliefs is wildly inconsistent with their common-sense perception of reality. When the conflict between the religious experience and the perception of reality is resolved by distorting the perception of reality, the price of the religious experience is very costly. We need to stand ready to assist these people in their transition to a religious experience that can be integrated with their common-sense perception of reality.

In my one year of clinical pastoral education at a juvenile detention center in Topeka, KS that was a part of the Menninger Foundation at the time, I interviewed a 16-year-old boy who had dreams of going into a lake that turned to blood and then fire. He had been raised in a Pentecostal church so there was no surprise on the part of the clinical director as to the source of his dysfunctional dreams and the treatment needed (which did not include a religious figure). This center, by the way, had a rate of recidivism of an unbelievably low 8% after two years of a boy leaving the center.

Fortunately, there are some newly evolving views of the Bible that should work just fine. Contemporary biblical criticism tries to understand the Bible in its historical context with all of its warts and allow us to get a sense of the divine. It opens us to the most profound struggles with the fundamental issues of life: what is the meaning of our lives, how do we endure pain, suffering and loss, how we can undo bad decisions, reverse unfortunate circumstances and find a sense of health, revitalization and hope. The Bible is a vehicle by which we can address these issues in a most productive way. We have to recognize, however, that the Bible will not provide any closed-form solutions; there are only the hints and the search for the answers.

Now to the heart of the ecclesiastical dilemma caused by the evolving view of scripture. Like any commercial enterprise, the church has to provide a product and the overwhelming temptation of the church is provide authoritative answers to the fundamental questions of life; even when there are no authoritative answers. In part, this explains why some cling tenaciously to an archaic view of the Bible; a view that does provide authoritative answers.

Thus, providing concrete products in the absence of an inspired Bible may be extremely difficult for the practitioners. On the one hand, we need to acknowledge that there are no simple answers to the ultimate questions of human life. On the other hand, we need to feel confident that there are solutions; albeit transcendental solutions and not necessarily ones that can quell our angst over our recognition of our own mortality.

The ecclesiastical dilemma stems from the fact that "transcendental solutions" are not a very marketable product line. As we cannot presume on what God might do or not do and that we cannot manipulate God through prayers, incantations or rites, we cannot deliver "ultimate solutions" with any commercially acceptable reliability.

We might start, however, by looking at how Jesus functioned and discover a way forward. The essence of his public ministry was to "encounter" the people of Canaan with an astute mixture of love, support, judgment and forgiveness. The profound result of those encounters was that many recognized that when they had met Jesus, that they had encountered the divine through him. This was sufficient by itself yet it seems, unfortunately, to have led his followers to forget about the "through him." and confer on him the appellation, "Son of God."

Despite the questionable emendations of the early records of Jesus public ministry and his elevation to all-man and all-god status, there is no question that he had a huge impact on the religious communities of Palestine. This may suggest that a productive direction to frame concrete products will be in the formation of transcendent relationships within the context of human unreliability. This will require appropriate safeguards and it is uncertain whether most pastors will possess an adequate level of skill. This, however, could be addressed by changes in seminary curricula. A more difficult but doable task would be the generation of a theological basis that will guide the movement and development of these communities and these relationships.

The real problem here is figuring out how to make a valid use of scriptures in support of ecclesiastical institutions (churches). This is not an impossible task but it is certainly way up on the hard-to-do list.

Most of the major religions including Christianity offer everlasting life and this goes away with a non-infallible Bible.

This need for concrete products should morph into meeting those needs that are attainable without a divinely inspired Bible and there are many including but not limited to:

- Forgiveness: this is usually framed in terms of the final judgement but it is much more important in the context of forgiving ourselves and being forgiven by those we have deeply hurt. Guilt is an exteremly powerful negative force that can lodge deeply in our psyches and even destroy lives through depression and alcoholism. It is possible for the practioners to unhook guilt through pastoral counseling, helping individuals develop strategies for atonement for those acts that they are unable to forive themselves or by verbal guidance from the pulpit. There may even be some merit in studying the dynamics of what takes place within what is called the confessional.

- Isolation: one of our greatest needs is overcoming a pervasive sense of loneliness spiked by our electronic world. A relevant cartoon is the couple eating together communicating to each other by text. The solution to our sense of isolation is not, however, the after service coffee but being guided in the dynamics of sharing ourselves in a way that results in feelings of oneness with others or at least connectedness. I dont see this present in most of our main stream protestant services nor in most Catholic masses but it is not impossible to inject such into these services. Some of this takes place within evangelical services but is marred by its adherance to an inerrant Bible. The path forward includes becoming open to the point of vulnerability and the ernest desire to immerse ourselves in others.

- Expanded Vision: all of us have experienced moments during services in which we transcend the ordinary and feel ourselves moving toward a higher plane. I find this most likely in services with chants and artistic constructs and less likely in the services centered in the reformed tradition that depend solely on the "Word of God" within churches with the more austere designs. Consider the power of Orff's O Fortuna-Carmina Burana in comparison to the traditional protestant hymns. Consider also the atonal calls to worship in Islam that resonate across the landsacpe and the involved motions of the faithful during prayers which are very annimated. In themselves, these produce a radical differentiation from the mundane that may assist the worshippers to reach beyond themselves.

- How We Relate. We are all in need of becoming a better spouse, parent, friend and person. Our ecclesiastical institutions, routed as they are in the life of Jesus, certainly could have a lot to say about ways to live better with others. The scriptures are not uniform in their guidance for better ways of living and in some cases we should have serious reservations about its guidance. In addition, a serious known problem is that some of those who express their religiosity the loudest are also some of the nastiest persons around. This, however, can be remedied by a skilled pastor to the benefit of the whole congregation by holding intimate discussions among the members.

- Hope. The aforementioned television pastor who made lavish promises in the name of God was on the right track. His goal was to provide hope to those on the edge of dispair. The cited problem with his approach was that there are no guarantees that some outside agent would be working on their behalf. This, however, is something that the collective resourses of a church could be mobilized to achieve. The requirements for doing this are many but at the center is the potential of the church's ministry to provide succor in our struggles with the vissitudes of life including our own mistakes. In addition and perhaps more important, the churches can be a major assist in helping parisioners moblize their own internal resources to address the problems they are confronting. This should not be in a "pull yourself up by your own bootstraps" approach but in laying out a strategy for a successful outcome.

- In Search of the Divine: When preparing a sermon properly, the preacher gets inside of the text and lets the text lead him into new avenues of thinking and an expansive awareness. He then, idealy, frames his message in a way that lifts his congregation into this expansive awareness. This is not easy but it is doable.

It seems clear that there are possibilities here but it is uncertain that these could be the basis of a church becoming an effective commercial activity. Yet it would be unfortunate to lose the churches as there are no other institutions in our societies that are dedicated to the betterment of the human condition. One might suggest that acadamia could step up and fill that bill but my experience has been that the main interest of most academics is in being seen by their colleagues as the most erudite.

During the height of the cold war, I was placed on a four person executive element of one of our three national continuity of government (COG) teams headed by a former Secretary of Defense. We had all of the right people from Defense, State, Intel and civil agencies and after three years of extensive exercises, we finally figured out what we were doing and became a national repository for the conduct of global nuclear war.[16] Near the end of this tenure, I sent myself to a meeting of the Society of Christian Ethics Committee on Nuclear War. I viewed myself as their customer and was hoping for insights that I could bring back to the three teams to expand our vision. Instead, the experience was a total waste. I spend the time listening to the academics trying to outdo each other in

16. One of the amazing things during this period of the cold war was that the overwhelming number of flag officers in the Pentagon with whom I worked viewed the sole purpose of our nuclear arsenal was deterrence. There was almost zero thought given to how do we fight a nuclear war and win.

their use of four syllable words. Sadly, in our search for alternative institutions to act toward the betterment of the human condition, it seems like we can pretty much rule out academia.

Another option might be our political parties but it is not clear that there ever has been a time in which their priorities placed the betterment of the human condition above staying in power. Yes, there are noted examples of exceptional individuals who genuinely sought the greater good but these are few. In addition, there are a number of not-for-profits and foundations that come close but their reach is so limited that it would be hard to place them at the forefront of this effort.

As a result, we may have to depend upon the churches as institutions that can help its members frame their value and behavioral systems but not in the traditional sense of looking for scriptural references that seem to fit strong biases such as with homosexuality as in 1 Corinthians 6:9 (". . . wrongdoers will not inherit the kingdom of God . . . nor men who have sex with men.") Equally in Sura 4:16, "If two men among you are guilty of lewdness, punish them both."

The irony, of course, at least with respect to Christianity, is that Paul's condemnations ran counter to Jesus central teaching embodied in the golden rule, "In everything do to others as you would have them do to you; for this is the law and the prophets (Matthew 7:12)." Jesus was correct in citing the golden rule as a counter to the often narrow precepts espoused by the religious practitioners of his time. He was rejecting these precepts and the authoritative guidance that filled scripture as to what are the "right" values and behaviors and what are the "wrong" ones.

Behavioral Systems

The golden rule provides guidance that addresses many but not most of the value and behavioral decisions we make every day. This is an outstanding mantra with which to live by when the decisions are pretty clear cut. For those decisions with multiple impacts, we may need a more robust criteria. Consider:

- Does the activity(ies) enhance our quality of life and that of our communities or

- Does the activity(ies) degrade our quality of life and that of our communities?

There are many activities for which a clear judgement is difficult and we can look at some of these. What we will find in several of these cases is that we are no closer to a clear answer than when we began. Examples include:

- Killing in war

- Abortion

- Sexual Function and Fidelity

- Lying

- Homosexuality

Let's apply the above criteria to see if it provides additional insights over the conventional approaches of examination.

Killing during War

This has produced "just war" tomes sufficient to fill small libraries. For the most part, these tomes proceed from various first principles and offer much erudition and little insight. We know that wars result from a combination of causes but are often instigated by an ambitions leader. While WW II was somewhat predictable given the Treaty of Versailles, it took a German leader to create the national fervor to propel Germany into its military actions. The watchword of many pacifists is the hope that by not supporting the leader they would prevent war. During my brief tenure as the head of the residue of the Civil Defense program, I had to deal with the then President of the Physicians for Social Responsibility who felt that supporting civil defense increased the likelihood of nuclear war. Both of these were based on grand wishes but not very sound reasoning.

The bottom line, of course, is that any war is a huge negative but sadly aggression must be met when the alternative is viewed as unacceptable. While it would be nice to reach some peaceful accommodation with the jihadists, this does not seem to be in the cards and killing becomes necessary. In another time, Churchill is alleged as preferring to lie dying in his own blood than to see the Swastika hanging down from the Westminster Palace. Thanks largely to the young pilots in the RAF, his decision not to make terms with Hitler was the right decision but the cost to England of that decision was enormous.

Where we need to be careful is when killing is raised to heroic standards. This is the mindset shown brilliantly in the movie "Patton." Worse was the preparations for the invasion of Japan near the end of the war in the Pacific. Our Generals and Admirals had been buoyed by the successes of their earlier invasions for which they were elevated to heroic standards (look at the multiple filming of MacArthur walking ashore in his return to the Philippines). Granted that most of the invasions in the South Pacific were necessary up to and perhaps Iwo Jima but certainly not Okinawa or the Japanese mainland. Even without the atomic bomb, it was totally unnecessary to invade Japan at an expected cost of a half million allied lives and many more Japanese. It is true that the Japanese viewed surrender as a loss of honor and its leadership resolved not to do so.

Notwithstanding, we could have simply sent our invasion forces home, made it clear to the Japanese leadership that we had no intention of a grand invasion and instead would fire bomb their cities until they quit. No honor for anyone. Yet, this option was never put on the table publicly or if it was, it was quickly squelched. In this case, the decisions had nothing to do with just war theory, the ethics of killing other human beings or the Ten Commandments but solely to do with the military inertia.

The options were very different in the 1940's England and Churchill knew the price England would have to pay in continuing to fight. Yet, he saw the other option as totally unacceptable. Sadly, as an RAF pilot stated after the war about one of the ME 109 pilots

he killed, "if we met on the street, we might have become friends."
No theories figure into to these decisions; only the options and
their impacts.

This is why the search for the divine is so critical. It is only
when we are able to see others from the same perspective that
Jesus advocated during his ministry that we can rise above the
perceived honors of militarism and seek vigorously other options
to the killing. Even when fighting on is the only tenable option, we
need to seek the least costly means.

Abortion

There is no rational criteria that can make sense out of this subject.
There is, however, a lot of condemnation that should go out to
those who recklessly get pregnant and then seek an abortion. The
thing that is not acceptable is the religious strictures that prevent
the use of the options that might prevent unwanted pregnancy.
The only thing that I can say beyond that is that I am glad that I
was not a "choice."

Sexual Function and Fidelity

This is the trickiest of the quandary issues because of the mytho-
logical status we place on sex. There are two distinct issues associated with this: a) function and b) fidelity.

There is, unfortunately, a distorted view of its function put
forth by practitioners from tribal to contemporary religions in
which sex is viewed solely as a means of procreation. It is true that
this is its biological function but it is also a potential source of
extreme pleasure for those who understand the means of giving
pleasure. Tragically, there are practitioners who weigh against this
even to the point of female gentile mutilation.

In addition, one of the major Christian religious communities insists the that the sole (underline sole) function of sex is
for procreation and only within marriage. This allows only the

so-called missionary position sex with other pleasurable practices often being cast as dirty or sinful. As a result of the latter, innumerable women and men have been and are being denied the connectedness that can be derived from a vital sexual experience.

Sexual fidelity is a bit trickier due to written and unwritten strictures defining the role of woman in a marriage. In the legitimate interest of the stability of the family, western and eastern religions have placed a premium on fidelity. This seems to have translated itself into notions of ownership of which the more extreme is that in Islam in which the hijab is prescribed as a garment "worn by women to maintain modesty and privacy from unrelated males" and to make certain a woman remains untouched by any other male than the one who owns her.

In the west, ownership is defined in terms of exclusive use. The unfortunate aspect of this is that the fundamental assumption underlying exclusive use is that each of the partners can meet 100% of the needs of the other. Whether this is even remotely possible or not is open for discussion but it appears that the "not" is a major factor in the dramatic divorce rates in the US.

Robert Heinlein, a great science fiction story teller, became the philosopher of inclusivity in his "Stranger in a Strange Land" [17]novel in which he challenged the assumptions and advocated treating sex no differently than having lunch with another person male or female. The downside to this view in the context of relationships is the strong possibility of the alienation of affections and the breakup of relationships. This is an understandable threat that is highlighted in a large portion of our county and western music themes that are expressions of the terrible pain of a broken relationship.

Clearly, a vital sexual relationship can be at the center of a relationship that lifts us beyond the mundane and provides glimpses of ourselves and a connectedness to another that can border on the transcendent. For this reason, we must figure out how to unhook ourselves from these dysfunctional strictures from the past.

17. Robert Heinlein, Stranger in a Strange Land, Ace/Putnam, 2005

John R. Powers

Lying

We need to distinguish the type of lying forbidden in the eighth commandment, "thou shalt not bear false witness against thy neighbor" from the common type of lying that is falsifying events for a personal need. The types of lying reflected in the commandment are mainly related to the courts and law enforcement and to a somewhat lesser extent slander.

The more common type of lying is that within relationships: child to parent, spouse to spouse, employee to employer, et al. There are clearly cases such as catastrophic medical news that telling the truth would be extremely harmful if the truth were told to persons really not ready for it. There is, however, a downside of lying in all such cases where the recipient suspected a lie and independently verified that it was a lie. In such a case, the word of the person telling the lie would be forever suspect.

This seems to be one of the major consequences of any lie as once trust is broken it is extremely difficult to repair it. Such The broken trust often leads to a broken relationship as the response to any subsequent query will be suspect even if it is wholly the truth. Parents love to believe that their kids always tell them the truth but once the kid is known to lie, the parents are likely to demand proof from them of future assertions on questionable issues.

Further, there is one additional factor that merits attention: the attitude of the recipient toward the truth. Many are the sad tales of persons in a relationship in which one of the partners encourages the other to tell the truth and then punishes the truth teller severely for the content of that truth. In some cases, it gets added to the "bag of hurts" and emerges again and again for years to come. Anyone asking for the truth needs to create an environment that accepts the truth. This may be extremely hard to do but it is essential if the recipient wants to hear the truth in all circumstances.

Homosexuality

This is such a bugaboo that it may be a good test of our efforts to establish constructs that enhance relationships rather than degrade them. We have seen the more destructive aspects of the biases against homosexuality. The Matthew Shepherd killing in Utah illustrates the psychotic internal wiring of the perpetrators that they would feel so threatened by gays that it would lead to such a vicious killing.

The potency of this threat is illustrated in the case of Kenneth Brewer and Stephen Bright.[18] Brewer met Bright at a local gay bar, bought Bright drinks and the two went back to Brewer's apartment. While there, Brewer made a sexual advance toward Bright and Bright beat him to death. A *gay panic defense* reduced the charges from second degree murder to assault. Clearly, Bright was aroused enough by the prospect of gay sex to be drawn into Brewer's apartment but then panicked when his arousal emerged into consciousness.

It seems reasonable to assert that the quality of life of gay individuals is enhanced by their freedom to follow their natural desires. American jurisprudence tends to side with the individual and has done so here recently with an amazing 7 to 2 decision by the Supreme Court to protect gays from being fired for being gay. The problem we seem to encounter is that some societies follow strictures that have absolute rights and wrongs.

Yet, these antiquated value and behavioral systems can be the source of immense individual and community harm. It is a mystery why these even exist when logic would dictate that our ethical and behaviors systems should be life enhancing. Pope Francis took a huge step forward in supporting same-sex civil unions but this still leave us with the huge issue of how can we then eliminate the negative strictures that we have inherited from the past?"

---

18. Jury tainted by homophobia? Star Bulletin, October 7, 1998

Eliminating Harmful Strictures from the Past

We need to look hard at those strictures especially those cited with scriptural authority or cloaked in the robes of tradition to see if they really make sense. It should be clear that many of these notions imbedded in people's heads can be extremely harmful if unquestioned. As a first step in their removal, we need to de-couple them from their supposed support in inerrant scripture or inviolate tradition. This is essential as both scriptures and tradition have provided succor to the purveyors of harmful ideas in ways that they use their personal hang-ups to spread misinformation. A classic was falsely crediting Pat Roberson with blaming CO-VID-19 on oral sex.

Closer to home, however, is the fact in the 40's my parents were so traumatized by talking about sex that I never received "The Talk" until I was 16 and then it was a five-minute version in which my mother told me that I should never touch a woman's breasts. The notion of sex as a way of giving pleasure must have been so foreign to them, that it never occurred to them to raise it nor to provide guidance on my primary responsibilities to satisfy the woman with whom I was engaged. I do not, however, fault them severely as this was the culture in which they were raised. This, however, is the point. No one expended the energy to elimi-nate these dysfunctional notions.

It was a culture that should have been excised as quickly as it emerged but it wasn't. Yet, the literature of the period suggested that sexual morays were as wide open as in any period of the late twentieth and early twenty-first centuries. It seems as if the stated values of the period were mostly superficial and had little to do with the behaviors. So, the question is twofold: a) what caused the disparity and b) why was this sustained? I have my suspicions but will pass on those and return to our main theme.

Our main focus is on an individual's search for the divine so why are harmful strictures relevant? These things not only get in the way of our search but they can do untold damage to our lives.

How do they get in the way of our search? The precepts that God is Love from 1 John 4:7 make that clear. There is no better way to search for the divine other than in relationships and most particularly in intimate relationships. Yet, there are strictures that prevent priests from having normal sexual relationships and the resultant horrific destruction of the lives of young children when the sexual needs of these priests become perverted. This barrier is furthered by the Vatican's teaching that the sole purpose of sex is procreation and the teachings of the more fundamentalist protestant Churches that paint some sexual practices as dirty and sinful thereby depriving the participants of a holy uplifting experience. Please hold that thought and we will return to this with a focus on approaches that are mutually fulfilling as challenges to those that are mutually-defeating.

We now need to take a brief look elsewhere at the worst hand me downs from previous generations that the US has ever experienced. The first is the systemic racism that has endured in this nation for four hundred years. It is pretty clear how African Americans became tagged with being a sub-human species given that they were torn away from their homes in Africa and put to work as chattel toiling in the fields under the burning sun. When slavery ended with the end of the civil war, most blacks were reduced to adject poverty with no way out thru a decent education and many were forced to work for their former overseers for a pittance and the majority of those who went north ended up with menial jobs at bare subsistence wages. As a result, an "intergenerational cycle of poverty" was created that continues to this day.

The worst part of this is that African Americans were and are living in a country with relative abundance and are able to see how little they have in comparison. This spawns the rage and criminality that is so often touted against them. It is regrettable but not surprising that legitimate protests supporting the rights of blacks end up getting laced with riots and looting.

Once blacks were defined as a sub-human species in the late 19th Century, a construct evolved that would define how they should behave in the company of white folks and any deviation from that would be met with the severest of measures. The most severe, of course, would be meted out to a black who was perceived to have looked lustfully at a white woman.

The real tragedy is that the children in all of these African American families craved a decent life. As the Chaplain at the Pennsylvania Youth Development Center in Philadelphia, I found the incarcerated black kids in my charge no different than kids in white neighborhoods who hungered for learning and love. These kids were given neither and were denied the developmental opportunities they needed to break free from the gang cultures in which most were immersed. As a result, the rate of recidivism was on the order of 75%. Thus, the intergenerational cycle of poverty is sustained.

We are not going to dwell on this other than to emphasize that each generation will need to figure out how to free itself from the toxic strictures handed down from previous generations. In above case, it may take the equivalent of a Minneapolis policeman kneeling on the neck of a black while he cries for his mama and tries to explain that he cannot breathe.

The issue here is solely "how do we overcome strictures from the past to rid ourselves of the attitudes and behaviors that are clearly harmful?" This is not easy as these are complex and deeply buried socially divisive issues. Some of these biases go to the core of the being of many people and when there are large numbers of like-minded peoples, they tend to reinforce the negative biases and perpetuate them. The delight in displaying confederate flags is a case in point and the adherence to being able to own assault weapons with no useful function is another. Both of these are fed by deep-seated emotional needs.

There is only one way I know to overcome harmful strictures from the past: personal awareness. For the most part, very few of those holding to the past will have any interest in changing their perceptions. It was somewhat an accident that I got to know blacks after being recruited to join an almost all black men's fast pitch softball team in the 1970's. As a result, my perceptions changed dramatically and I found lifelong friends among them.

This, however, is not very helpful when applied to the anti-black demonstrators at Charlottesville nor the AK-47 totters who marched up the steps of the Michigan governor's office demanding that she end the COVID-19 restrictions. Neither of these groups had any interest in looking at life from a different perspective. The tragic irony here is that many of these people consider themselves good Christians.

Our goal here, however, is not to correct socially dysfunctional attitudes but search for the divine. We must first, unfortunately, cleanse ourselves of these dysfunctional attitudes if we hope to succeed.

Encountering the Divine

There are many pathways to encountering the divine. A most promising one begins with a strong desire to become the person we would like ourselves to be. When we head down this path, however, it does involve a bit of risk as we really don't know very much about the divine and have no idea where we are going. As a result, the old saw. "I'll know it when I see it" doesn't apply.

Each of our lives is a journey and for the most part, we must settle down into a mundane routine that is necessary to feed, clothes and house ourselves and those for whom we have responsibilities. With this in mind, encountering the divine can put us on a path in which we get a sense that we have gone awry with a need for a radical change that could lead to a sense of "standing alone in front of the abyss" as suggested by Ernest Becker who was echoing the refrain that is the culmination of a long line of existentialists from Kierkegaard to Rank.[19]

This, however, is overstated and the outcome may not be as dire as Becker might suggest. Yet, it should not be understated either. When we search for the divine, we are opening ourselves up to change; possibly radical change. The impact of this is to put everything about ourselves on the table including what the

19. Ernest Becker, Op Cit.

existentialists would call an inauthentic existence. Will this then lead to abandoning our current lifestyle and devoting ourselves to our search for the ultimate? Maybe yes and maybe no.

This was certainly the case with Jesus and his disciples. While it is true that the texts of the four Gospels were oft emended and redacted, the basic thrusts of Jesus' teachings are clear. He was a reformer of radical dimensions who advocated a way of life that was so extreme that only a Gandhi like person would be able to even approximate what Jesus was asking.

It is pretty hard to read the New Testament and the Gospels especially without coming away with this realization. Many times, as a late teen and early twenty something, I listened to sermons taken from the Gospels and felt woefully short of what was demanded. So, to repeat, should we then abandon all else and devote ourselves with a consuming a search for the ultimate (which, translated here, would mean following Jesus)?

This wasn't that satisfying in the case of Hesse's Siddartha whose life was a frustratingly endless search without recognizing that he had attained what was possible; a series of enlightening insights.[20] His sense of failure, however, arose because he never achieved what he thought he sought: a life consuming experience in which he achieved a "oneness with the universe" or, alternatively, in Buddhist terms, Nirvana. Siddartha experienced the divine in many different ways but appears to have had no idea what he was seeking nor did he have any idea when he found aspects of it. This was the crux of his problem and is the crux of our problem.

Our heads have been so screwed up by the images promulgated by the practitioners that we may never be able to free ourselves. While images such as "God the Father" are comforting, there is no basis for these images and even less for the accompanying notion that God has a plan for each of us and will see us thru our troubles. The later followers of Jesus seem to have put forward the contrary notion that God will watch over us and see us through our most difficult troubles by asserting in the canonical gospels, "Don't fret about your life . . . birds of the sky . . . lilies of the field . . . won't God

20. Herman Hesse, Op Cit

care for you even more (Matthew 25–30)." While this is deeply comforting, it cannot be supported by any observation of human experience. There is no heavenly being out there watching over us and assuring that we will have a fulfilling life. If we are to make progress in our journey, we need to shed ourselves of these images and notions and accept the fact that we are the searchers and we are the agents and we are subject to the vicissitudes of human existence.

The divine is much more elusive than these conventional images portray. Yet, all is not lost. We are not alone. There are many real persons close to us and we need to reach out and connect meaningfully. The key word here is meaningfully.

In many ways we are just like the kid who ventures out to explore her or his immediate neighborhood and then wanders farther to discover the greater world beyond. We will never come to the end of our search but we will continuously be amazed and enlightened by our discoveries along the way including the interactions with those with whom we truly connect.

Another way of thinking about this is that we must see what is over the next hill. The search for the divine is, of course, a much more intense enterprise than simply a geographic curiosity. It can become a part of our life's blood and as all-consuming as in Siddhartha's search. At a minimum, most if not all of us long for emotional connections that are a lot better than the ones we are experiencing. The reason that our connections lack what we would like is a combination of how we are using ourselves and circumstance. We may not have much influence over circumstance but we can reflect on how we are using ourselves in our relationships.

This longing for enhanced emotional connections is something we may feel throughout our lives and the lack thereof will often lead to bitterness. In this regard, again, we can see the truth in Augustine's famous quote, ". . . our hearts are restless till they find their rest in thee."[21] It appears that this is a condition that is near universal in that we all have a patently obvious inherent restlessness. We know that there is something fundamentally lacking

21. Augustine, *Confessions of Saint Augustine*, 1.1.1.

in our lives but just can't put our finger on exactly what it is. For the most part, we do a pretty good job at burying this amongst the daily routines but there is still a residual emptiness that persists.

The tragedy of our contemporary worship services is that most of us attend with the hope of filling that emptiness but walk away frustrated and empty. Think about why that is. The answer is complex but the main reasons are that the services are not focused realistically on our real and immediate needs. Yet, these services can provide an environment in which something extra-ordinary can occur.

In this environment, we can be lifted out of ourselves in a way to see the whole of life from a different perspective; we see ourselves with a different lens; and we can touch the soul of another person in a way that we are transformed. Again, we should put some trust in the 1 John 4:7–21 theme that begins, "let us love one another, for love is from God, and whoever loves has been born of God and knows God" and continues in v 12, "No one has ever seen God; if we love one another, God abides in us and his love is perfected in us." While this contains some parochial phrases such as, "whoever confesses," the central thrust is valid.

This sounds easy but it is anything but. We are not talking about snuggling in bed with our favorite partner. We are talking about giving of ourselves and this can lead to pretty radical turns. We can begin by taking mini steps in that direction every day and by doing so feel an expansiveness that is unlike our everyday experiences. Yet, it will draw us into seeking even more such experiences.

One such mini step occurred when I was in a small Asian restaurant with a female friend and as I was getting our food from the counter, I noticed an elderly woman sitting at a nearby table who had a handful of small change and was counting and recounting it without ordering. After setting down our food on our table, I took a twenty out of my wallet and asked my friend to give it to the women. Yes, it gave me a moments rush but then afterward I regretted not giving her all of the hundred and twenty dollars that was in my wallet at the time.

Assuming that she was not playing me (my skeptical self might ask), this was a personal failure as she needed the hundred and twenty a lot more than I did. This epitomizes for me the heart of Matthew 25:35–36 that reads, "For I was hungry and you gave me something to eat, I was thirsty and you gave me something to drink, I was a stranger and you invited me in, I needed clothes and you clothed me, I was sick and you looked after me, I was in prison and you came to visit me." Forget the fact that this is in the context of earning a pass during the final judgment (presumably a later addition). This theme represents a central teaching of Jesus, which imposes on each of us a duty to those who are not in good circumstances.

When we are able to rise above our narrow personal interests and give of ourselves, we can open a gateway to the transcendent. If we could perpetuate such a state, we might be able to discover what is meant by the kingdom of god on earth. The barrier that makes it difficult for all of us non-Gandhi types is that we quickly become consumed not only by our daily chores of providing for our food, clothing and lodging but soon cross the threshold where our priorities expand to include the best of luxury vacations, private schools for the kids, the latest fashions and fancy cars.

It is these needs that create some of the impediments that get in the way of experiencing the divine. Once we get into the acquisitions cycle, we accumulate debt and debt is a vicious mistress. Eventually it will wear us down. In addition, the acquisitions themselves become an end game and obscure our needs for a more fulfilling life through enhanced relationships. It becomes even worse when we begin to see our self-worth in terms of our acquisitions.

Once this occurs, it will inevitably trigger our competitive juices. Competition, on the one hand is a huge plus as it can push us to excel at what we can personally produce and is the foundation of the western economies. We all witnessed the dysfunction in the socialist eastern European economies under communism in the second half of the 20th Century.

While competition has these huge economic benefits, on the other hand, it stirs in us the desire to be better than. This is at the heart of the racism that found its symbols in the Jim Crow laws that were rampant throughout our society until repealed. Sadly, the mindsets that spurred them still exist.

The destructive aspect of the "better than" form of competition runs deep. We find it among men and women chatting aimlessly seeking to put down others as a way of feeling good about themselves. It is depressing when this emerges during the after-worship coffee conversations among the most righteous in the congregation and in Christmas letters whose sole purpose is to say "look at me and what I and my family have accomplished." I had a member of our condo board in Ocean City NJ who could not stop telling me how much she does for her church.

We could expand this list of impediments but that is unnecessary. The general impact of these behaviors is to move us more toward self-isolation. If we can agree that any behavior that further isolates us is a hindrance to encountering the divine then the path forward becomes clearer: shed all of the toxins that stand between ourselves and others. Resolve to help make others feel good about themselves and their circumstances.

The Way Forward

Shedding the toxins that stand between ourselves and others is the most critical step in being able to embrace the divine. The difficulty is in identifying our toxins? One way is to experiment during our encounters with others is by listening intently with a goal of really connecting with that person and then making a mental note of everything we do that gets in the way. Videotaping would be great but that would alter the conversation itself. Notwithstanding, if that is the only way to get a handle on our self-destructive interpersonal behaviors then do it.

Among these toxins, the foremost are a) touting our own accomplishments, b) trying to sound brilliant and c) giving advice prematurely (my girlfriend keeps telling me "Just listen . . . don't try to solve the problem"). At the outset, it may be hard to constrain ourselves but if we really are interested in the other person, we will find a way thru the maze and be able to see life from the other's perspective. In the process, we just might get a glimpse of the divine.

There are techniques for connecting deeply to others found under the heading of "active listening." Accomplishing a deep connection, however, is much more than mastering techniques. It requires a changed mindset from self to other. For a brief moment, it is possible to live as a part of the other and with each such experience, we can expand our grasp of the divine and create a foundation that will open us to an even greater sense of being.

Every time we connect with another on a deeply personal level, we expand who we are in ways we can barely imagine. There are, however, limits to how deeply we can or should connect to others set by who we are and who they are. One of the ground breaking psychiatrists, Robert Lindner took the concept of Carl Rogers' Client Centered Therapy to its extreme limit by actually entering into the psychotic states of his patients and then working inside these states with the patients. Between them they engineered their way out.[22] This was brilliant but a bit risky.

Another caution is where the needs of the other are so great that identifying with them can totally deplete one's resources and then possibly make things worse by initially implying commitment and then not meeting the created expectations. In such cases, it is critical to be fully aware of your limits before you connect so you do not imply more that you are able and ready to give.

Yet, there is a significant role for less-than-fully-vested connections. I have found such connections to be extremely fulfilling. As mentioned previously, I played ball in Southeast Washington DC where the personal, educational and financial needs were overwhelming. If I had the ability to feed the five thousand, I might make a dent in this but I don't and it is important that I realize that I don't.

22. Robert Lindner, The Fifty-Minute Hour, Other Press, 1999.

Notwithstanding, this cannot diminish my responsibility to the many persons I encounter before, during and after the games. We can always take a moment to let those we meet know that "you are important." The amazing thing about my doing this is that the return I received was many times my investment. After a couple of years on Sunday afternoons in Anacostia, I would be greeted with "hi's" from the stoops along Summer Road, SE. I cherish those moments. I had become a part of the neighborhood and in becoming part of the neighborhood I was sharing in the divine presence.

By now it should be clear that the search for the divine is not done mostly by kneeling on a prayer bench in a church sending petitions to a Father above. Unfortunately, there is no one on the receiving end of these petitions despite the eons of assertions provided by the practitioners. The same can be said for prayers to the Virgin or the Saints or lighting candles for the same reason. This is not to reject prayer as an act of reaching for the beyond but it is to reject prayer as a way of soliciting action from an entity on high.

From this perspective, we need to view the sacraments from the right perspective. They do not do anything in the sense of desired outcomes. They can, however, focus us on the beyond. Paul Tillich's concept of "symbol" is pertinent here as a "symbol that participates in the reality to which it points."[23]

The mystics, on the other hand, would have us search the void for a connection to the divine. This notion reflects our intuitive sense that there is a differentiation between ourselves and the other and perhaps this should not be dismissed blithely. In some sublime sense, this is what happened to me while camped at 17,800 feet in the Himalayas. Gazing at the immense expanse of the universe on a night with no moon and no outside lights was a life changing experience.

So how do we wrap up this discussion? We don't! We know that there is more to existence then our own consciousness and that spurs us to search outward. We have no idea what we are seeking in terms of the divine nor any surety when we have encountered it

23. Paul Tillich, Op Cit.

but we sense that it is there. What we do know is the search for the divine is a part of life's journey. This is sufficient.

Epilogue

Since I have put so much weight on interpersonal communications as the way to experience the promise of 1 John 4:7 (. . . love one another . . . everyone who loves . . . knows God), let me share a few insights that I gathered from a multitude of experts on the ways to improve communications even to the point of becoming vested in others and experiencing life from their perspectives.

We begin by working to understand other people's view of the world; their interests, feelings and values. In order to move in this direction, if we have not done so already, we must gain the acceptance and trust of others. We can do this by:

- Focusing on the other person and use our body to say I'm listening
- Making the other person feel valued
- Asking open ended non-threatening questions
- Using statements that reflect back what the other person is saying and feeling (you seem perplexed; you would like your parents to trust you more)
- Avoiding leading, teaching, giving advice or boosting yourself.
- Conveying interest and respect

There are many books on the subject of active listening so I will just leave this as a something for the reader to pursue at leisure. The importance of mastering these techniques cannot be overstated and I hope that you will become a devotee. In that regard, I will cite one endorsement for the techniques I learned after I digested them and created a two-day course on Communications, Negotiations and Conflict Resolution. After providing the course to the senior professional staff at the DC Courts in 2002, one of the participants emailed me afterward with the comment, "this course saved my marriage."

For all of that, however, mastering the techniques in all of the books, pales in comparison with a deep desire to really connect to another person.

Synopsis

WE OFTEN EXPERIENCE A profound longing for a spiritual connection beyond ourselves. This is best expressed in Augustine's "our heart is restless until it finds its rest in thee." We sense that there is a something missing in our lives but have a hard time putting our finger on exactly what it is.

Herman Hesse's *Siddhartha* is a great illustration of the search for spiritual fulfillment without a firm conclusion. Siddhartha tried many different pathways and touched on what he sought many times but did not recognize what he had achieved. We likewise seek to fill this longing in different ways. The most common is through religious institutions but, sadly, these efforts have become increasingly disappointing for many due largely to unsubstantiated claims made from the pulpits about the Scriptures. Yet, these Scriptures represent a treasure trove of insight garnered over the centuries if read for what they represent.

In Search of the Divine does not pretend to be able to provide a roadmap to a definitive search but it does provide hints that can lead to an expanded vision and connections to the transcendent.

Author Bio

JOHN POWERS IS A national security and emergency management consultant currently assisting DC Fire and EMS to develop a mass casualty response plan. Previously, he led a joint private sector-interagency effort to reduce the risk of nuclear terrorism and served as the Executive Director of the President's Commission for Critical Infrastructure Protection and as a FEMA Regional Director. Earlier, John commanded a Marine Corps Reserve Attack Squadron. John holds an MDiv from Princeton Theological Seminary and a PhD in physics from the University of Pennsylvania.

CPSIA information can be obtained
at www.ICGtesting.com
Printed in the USA
BVHW081155170921
616981BV00007B/164